# HAVE A GRAND & GLORIOUS DAY

Observations from a simple man

BRETT NEIL

# HAVE A GRAND & GLORIOUS DAY

Observations from a simple man

---

Copyright © 2020 by Brett Neil

Printed and Electronic Versions
ISBN: 978-1-7340250-1-9
(Brett Neil /Motivation Champs)

All rights reserved. No part of this book may be reproduced or transmitted in any form or by any means, electronic or mechanical, including photocopying, recording, or by any information storage and retrieval system, without permission in writing from the copyright owner.

The book was printed
in the United States of America.

To order additional copies or bulk order contact the publisher, Motivation Champs Publishing.
www.motivationchamps.com

While reading *Have a Grand and Glorious Day*, it is my hope that you will be able to let go of your past baggage and start a new path that will allow you to relax and enjoy your time here on earth! This book covers 11 basic areas of life that every human being will have to deal with at some time or another. I hope it will make you laugh, cry and make changes if needed. It is fairly short and sweet, and is not designed to be an end all book. Although some chapters may not need much more expounding, I already have ideas for future books or posts for other chapters. I know that if you will read this book and apply what you read it will change your life. Read it and share it. As Mr. Roger's once said, "We are all called to be repairers of creation." These truths can literally change the world if we apply them.

# Introduction

As I travel around I find few people who are fulfilled and content with their lives. Most are looking for something. They're not sure what but they know there has to be a better way to live. They are good people who have been left empty by the "I want more and I want it now way of life."

We live in a society that is somewhat spoiled. Convinced that much of what is wrong in the world and in our lives is someone else's fault we become offended when others disagree with us or challenges our opinion. Our kids expect a trophy or ribbon just because they participate. We have forgotten (some may have never known) that hard work and failing are synonymous with success.

I realize that many of us have been dumped on and deeply hurt by others. I am not making light of this; please know I feel your hurt. I have been hurt deeply and I have hurt others deeply. I am not a saint nor do I pretend to be. Many a time in my life I have been a total screw up. One of the reasons I am writing this book is to help us take control of our own lives, let go of the past and look to the future. If we don't, we are going to live a life filled with depression and frustration.

I have discovered that by surrendering my hurts and pain to God and letting Him change my heart and mind I can enjoy life even in the midst of trials.

Have a Grand and Glorious Day were typically the last words my youngest son would hear from me when I would drop him off at school. No matter how our morning had gone, I wanted him to believe it was possible to make the best of the day and enjoy life. I want everyone I meet to know a Grand and Glorious Day is possible!

# Chapter One
## WE CAME WITH A GUIDE BOOK

The First step to living a Grand and Glorious life is realizing that you are not an accident. You didn't come from a monkey. You were created by God. There is a God who loves you. The Bible says he knew us before we were in our mother's womb. He gave us a book to help us know how to relate to Him. It is not meant to be a rule book but rather a book to show us how rules keep us from Him.

I personally don't like to read manuals. I like to figure it out on my own. Problem is many times I don't get the full benefit out of the product I am using.

A few years back some dear friends gave me a range finder. It is designed to tell you how far you are from a golf hole so you will know which club to use. I was excited; however, it didn't seem to work nearly as well as the ones my playing partners were using. After a while I quit using it. This summer, my oldest son was in from Colorado and we were able to play golf several times. He asked me where my range finder was, so I got it out and charged it up. I explained to him that it was only capable of performing a few basic functions and the battery lasted just a few holes. He took it with us anyway. Turns out, there was a guidebook built into the software. By the second hole he figured out I had something set wrong. After that it did more than I could have imagined and the battery would last for two full rounds. For two years I had told people that this was an inferior product. Turns out there was nothing wrong with the GPS; I was just failing to follow the Guidebook.

I believe this is the same problem with people. We are not an inferior product. We just function poorly because we have forgotten to check the Guidebook. We are getting our instructions from instructors that never read the manual or have read it and missed the message of it altogether.

The Bible is separated into two parts. The Old Testament and the New Testament. The Old Testament shows us what life is like when we choose to live by religion, laws and rules. The New Testament shows us what life is like under grace when we accept that Jesus came to set us free from religion. The Old Testament was written to the Jewish people and for us. It is the story of the old covenant between God and Israel. It follows a "you do your part and I'll do mine" system. Much of Jesus teaching was to show the people under the old covenant why He came to establish the new covenant. Paul refers to Jesus as a minister of circumcision. (Romans 15:8) Under the law of rules it might be necessary to poke your eyes out to keep you from lusting but not under the law of grace. It is very important we don't try to live under both covenants but sadly that is exactly what most Christians try to do. I know this will be controversial but living by the letters in red will in many cases keep you under the law and away from grace. In the New Testament we are introduced to the new covenant between Father, Son and Spirit. God does His part and our part. The old covenant was given to us to show us that following a set of rules is not only impossible for us but is also not what God is interested in at all. He wants relationship with us. Romans 5:7 tells us that the law actually caused us to sin. Tell a 3 year old what not to do and see what he does! We have a tendency to view God as an angry father who can't look at us because we can't seem to follow the rules. God is a loving Father who is anguished (not angry) by our sin because it hurts us, not because it hurts Him or separates us from Him (Romans 8:28,). Jesus referred to God as Papa! This is hardly the term you would use for an angry old man who didn't like us! The phrase "For His mercy endures forever" appears 26 times in Psalms 136. Every sentence of that chapter ends with that phrase. Remember this is Old Testament stuff. Still God was telling us, don't be scared of me, learn to see me and my amazing grace.

George McDonald once said "To say on authority of the Bible that God does a thing no honorable man would do, is to lie against God; to say that is therefore right, is to lie against the very spirit of God." Never doubt that God loves you. "God the Father is like Jesus. Exactly like Him."

I encourage you to read the bible daily. I also encourage you to ask Jesus to teach you as you read. Remember, Jesus is the only infallible, inerrant, living word of God. The Bible is very clear about that. The Bible is intended to point us to Jesus and The Father, to help us see our Father's mercy and grace toward all people. Anytime you read something in the Bible that appears to contradict the teachings of Jesus, ask Him to reveal the truth to you. Don't try to combine old covenant teachings with new covenant teachings. Remember that most of the teaching of Jesus was done to people that were still under the old covenant. It wasn't until His death on the cross that the new covenant went into effect. Just as I have a will that goes into effect when I die, the will of Jesus went into effect when He died. That's why He could say "When I am lifted up I will drag all the peoples to myself!" John 12:32 (The Greek word normally translated as draw is much better represented in the word drag.)

Jesus said, "I and my Father are one... "If you have seen me you have seen the Father."

Don't ever believe for a minute that Jesus came to protect you from the Father. He came to introduce you to His Father. Remember "God is light and in Him is no darkness at all!" 1 John 1:5. The Pharisees knew the Bible that existed at that time from cover to cover. They had the Torah memorized, yet Jesus told them that although they knew the book, they did not know the Father. That can probably be said of many religious people today.

It's interesting that there were over 600 laws in the Old Testament and Jesus summed them up in two! "Love the Lord your God with all your heart, mind and soul and love your neighbor as yourself." The first question that comes to my mind is that if I love God with ALL my heart, mind and soul what is there left to love my neighbor with? Peter Hiett suggests, that the only way this is possible is if "God actually dwells in all of us." When we realize this we are able to love God in them even though they may not realize yet that He is in them. Jesus said, "At that day you will know that I am in My Father, and you in Me, and I in you."

If you're new to reading the Bible, I would encourage you to start by reading the eBook Unlock your Bible by Steve McVey. Read the book of Proverbs and the gospel of John. Proverbs has 31 chapters, one for each day of the month. It is full of practical wisdom about how to live life. The Gospel of John presents the Good News of Jesus in the clearest manner of all the New Testament books. Although there are many verses of great promise in John, two in particular speak the Good News to me. John 3:35 "The Father loves the Son and has given ALL things into His hand." And John 6:39 "This is the will of The Father who sent me, that of ALL He has given me I should lose nothing, but should raise it up at the last day!" Ignore anyone who tries to tell you God loves some but looks forward to punishing others for eternity. Trust Jesus and His promise to "Make all things new." Another great book of the Bible to read is the Psalms, it is full of worship, praise and promise!

## Chapter Two
## WE ALL HAVE FAITH IN SOMETHING

The second step to a Grand and Glorious Life is to realize that there will always be things that don't make sense, things that you cannot explain. No matter how smart we may be (or think we may be) some things just can't be explained without faith.

We all live with faith in something. Those who don't believe God created the world but believe it all happened by chance through the "Big Bang Theory" do so by faith. Since this theory can't be duplicated or observed it has to be accepted by faith that all of the energy in the universe gathered into one small dot the size of a period, which then exploded, bringing total unity out of total chaos. Try putting a hand full of metal and glass in a paper bag and blowing it up, if you end up with a Rolex we'll talk!

Evolution is another popular teaching that must be accepted by faith. The science and evidence used to support the theory of evolution is absent one key element, the missing link. If we evolved, why did it stop? How many people with tails have you seen swinging around through trees on their way to catch the latest movie? Again, you have to accept this theory by faith.

I believe God created the heavens and the earth. I believe He created man in His image. Even though I don't understand everything there is to know about God, I accept by faith that as I look around there must be something far greater than man and science to make all of this happen. "Both the Holy Scriptures and

Nature proceed from the divine word (Jesus)!" Galileo Galilei.

When God gave the Ten Commandments to the nation of Israel they didn't make sense to them. They had been in captivity for hundreds of years. They were forced to work 7 days a week and had been treated like animals yet somehow they trusted God enough to try them. They believed that if they followed them they would begin to understand their benefit. That's why they were able to say "we will do and we will understand."

In the end, we all must realize that life is a journey of trust, not a journey of understanding. As we learn to trust God more, we understand more, but we will never understand everything until we stand before the Creator. Until then, strive to learn but be okay with not knowing everything. Focus on what we do know. The rest will fall into place.

# Chapter Three
# TWO KEY WORDS

Kindness and truth: these two words will help us go far in living a "Grand and Glorious Life". Be kind to everyone who comes into your life. Being kind is something everyone can do and it doesn't cost us anything. Tell the truth. Be honest. Do it with kindness, but do it. We all feel uplifted when someone is kind to us.

"Be kind to each other, tenderhearted, forgiving one another, just as God through Christ has forgiven you." Ephesians 4:32

I have never met anyone who didn't like to be treated kindly. Have you ever had someone be kind to you? Think about how that made you feel. Start being kind today. Open the door for someone. Give up your seat. Tell them how nice they look. How much you appreciate them. Few things affect us more positively than kindness.

Be truthful with those around you. Share how you feel; don't harbor bad feelings. Deal with issues as they arise. The longer you allow things to fester the worse they get. Most problems start small and grow out of control only because we don't talk it out.

We live in a society where truthfulness is rare. Politicians lie to us to get elected, researchers lie to us to get grants, advertisers lie to us to sell products, and unfortunately, we lie to each other to get what we want out of relationships. In the end, lies destroy but truth prevails.

By learning to deal with others in kindness and truth we can build strong, long-lasting relationships. You cannot have a Grand and Glorious life without great relationships.

The very nature of God is relational. The Father, the Son and the Holy Spirit are always working together in unison with one purpose: to be in fellowship with us.

The Greek word used to describe this relationship is - Perichoresis (Mutual indwelling without the loss of personal identity.) Perichoresis was a dance in which 3 people weaved in and out with each other going faster and faster in a flowing motion. As the early church fathers observed this dance they felt it best described the relationship of the Father, Son and Holy Spirit. God wants us to know He dwells in us and we in Him (John 14:20). This is also how a marriage should be. We become one unit working together without losing our personal identity. This can't happen without kindness and truth.

My wife and I just celebrated 40 years of

marriage. It has been great but it is not always easy. We do our best to never go to bed angry with each other. Sometimes, we must agree to disagree. But always, we try to treat each other with kindness and truth. Sometimes the truth hurts, but when delivered with kindness it is much better received than when it is blurted out in anger. I never go to sleep without thanking God for her and asking Him to bless her and keep her safe. Fight fair, be kind, be truthful, learn to laugh at yourself, and your marriage will be a blessing!

## Chapter Four
## LEARN TO GIVE

As I mentioned earlier, I believe we have been created in God's image. The original text in Genesis reads "And Elohim (God), the great powerful one, filled the man with representation of Himself."(Ancient Hebrew Research Center) Being made in His image doesn't mean we look like Him, it means we were created to be like Him, act like Him, love like Him, forgive like Him and give like Him.

God is love and God's nature is to give. John 3:16 states that "For God so loved the world that He gave himself (through Jesus) in order for us to have an eternal relationship with him".

The most important part of learning to love is to learn to give. The giver always loves more than one who receives. Oftentimes, the receiver takes for granted the gift they have been given. Giving is probably the number one way we can reflect the image of God to others.

Learn to give. Give at least 10% of your after tax income. God calls this the tithe. In Deuteronomy 14:23 we are told that God established the tithe to teach us to fear Him. A much better translation of the word fear would be "to see Him." Proverbs 1:7 tells us that the beginning of wisdom is fear of God. When we give, we begin to see God working in areas we didn't notice Him before. As we see Him, we begin to gain wisdom. In Malachi 3:10, God promises that if we tithe, we have the right to expect Him to open the windows of Heaven and bless us with all we need. Finally in Malachi 3:11, He promises to protect the 90% we have left and to protect our income source.

Understand, I am not saying you must give to be "saved" or that giving will put you in better standing with God. I am telling you that giving will change your life because it will change your attitude towards others. Give of your time, your money and your talents, and it will be given back to you according to Jesus. Don't miss this. Become a giver!

Over and over in the Bible we are instructed to give to the poor. I don't believe you can ever be happy in life until you learn to give at least 10% of your income. Although you may think that you can't afford to give, I know from experience you can't afford not to. I really believe that learning to give is that important. Some will tell you this has to be to the local church. Although I do tithe to my church, I also give to many other needs as well. Ask God where you should give.

1 Timothy 6:17-19 are great verses to help us learn to give. Personalizing scripture oftentimes helps the words become part of me, this is a great example, "Teach me Lord not to be proud and trust in my money, which is so unreliable. Let my trust be in God who gives me all I need for my enjoyment. I will be rich in good works and generous to those in need, I will always be ready to share with others. By doing this I will be storing up treasure as a firm foundation for the future so that I may experience life that is truly life."

Learning to give is perhaps the most important step to a Grand and Glorious Life.

## Chapter Five
## WHERE DID THAT COME FROM?

Learn to expect God's favor. Once we begin to respect God, give, be kind and truthful, then we need to learn to expect God's favor. In the Bible, God promises to bless us when we follow him. I'm not telling you He will make you rich. I am promising He will make your life full and blessed. He will give you purpose. In John 10:10 Jesus told us that he came to give us life and that (life) more abundantly.

God loves His children more than we love ours. He wants good for us. He knows that by giving and serving we will learn to love. Because of that He can give us more because

He knows He can trust us to use it wisely. 2 Chronicles 16:9 tells us that the "eyes of the Lord run to and fro looking for people to bless."

As God blesses us, we in turn are to bless others even more. Somehow we have allowed ourselves to believe we should feel guilty when we are blessed. The only time we should feel guilty about being blessed is if we are not using the blessing we receive to help others.

When we give, we will be blessed. This applies to money, jobs, and relationships. "Give and it shall be given to you. Pressed down, shaken and running over shall men give to you" Luke 6:38. This is a law as strong as gravity. Give your time, your money, and your love. It will definitely lead to a Grand and Glorious Life.

Please understand that I am not saying because you give you will never suffer or that you will become rich. Jesus gave all He had while here on earth and it got Him killed! There is a difference between being fulfilled and having material possessions. The blessing I am referring to is when Jesus told the woman at the well about living water, which offers fulfillment and peace that passes all understanding. I give not because I have to and not for a reward, but because Jesus gave, and He asked me to imitate Him. I know of people that follow this principle of giving that are not yet believers, but they still experience the same results. Personally, I believe that is because God honors His word no matter the person's belief system. When we give to those who can't repay without expecting a reward we are acting like God. He is living in us and working through us. This is one of those "God works in mysterious ways" moments!

## Chapter Six
## I CAN'T AFFORD THAT!

Stay out of debt. Debt is the number one reason for marriage problems. Debt cripples most of us. None of us need a $30,000 car we are making payments on. Stop borrowing money for things you don't need.

Debt is why we are broke. I have heard Dave Ramsey say on his radio show that the average person owes $15,000 on credit cards, $26,000 on car loans, and $47,000 on student loans. Learn to buy only what you can pay for in cash.

Stop getting student loans to live on. Get a job. Throw papers, deliver pizzas, work. It is possible to work your way through college. Go to a junior college or community college. Do whatever it takes to avoid graduating with a large student loan. According to Nerd Wallet each year, millions of dollars in scholarships and grants go unused because students are too lazy to apply for them.

Start today by reading "The Total Money Makeover" by Dave Ramsey. Create a budget outlined in the book. Stick to it! Do the "debt snowball". Listen to Dave's show on his podcast called *Don't Look Back*. You can change your Legacy!

We cannot give because we are broke. We cannot enjoy what we have because we are broke. We are broke because we can't say no to buying stupid stuff we don't need.

STOP IT NOW!!!

I don't want to be too harsh, but it is important that you get this. Debt ruins our lives. It controls us. It burdens us. It wears us down.

Jesus came to set us free. Once we realize that He has freed us from the burden of sin we are able to relax and enjoy life. Getting out of debt frees us also. Make becoming debt free a priority. We are so blessed to live in a nation where we are free to work and build wealth. Do you want to make a difference in the world? Get out of debt, build wealth, and use it to help others do the same. The government can only build wealth for the politicians who run it. Hard working, debt free men and women can help build wealth for the whole society.

Debt on depreciating items (cars, TV's, engagement and wedding rings, vacations) has a double negative effect. Not only are we paying more (because of interest) for something, we also end up owing more than something is worth once depreciation sets in. Avoiding debt is hard because we are bombarded with commercials and ads designed to suck us in. Our elected officials borrow money every day to provide programs we don't need to get votes so they can get rich at our expense. Don't be lured in. There are few things more freeing than not having debt and few things more draining than being in debt. You can become debt free. I have attached several helps at the end of this book. Determination is the main thing needed to succeed! I pray you will decide to make it happen!

# Chapter Seven
## IT'S MY FUTURE

---

Put aside 10% of your income for yourself. Live for today but plan for the future. Be disciplined about saving. Start as soon as you pay off your debt. This will allow you to help others. It will also give you the ability to take care of yourself instead of relying on the government when you get older.

Having some money put aside is always better than being broke. You can leave something for your kids and grandkids, take care of your parents, and help a charity. Money in the bank is always better than being broke and in debt.

Having money will open doors to make more money. Make sure you possess it. Don't let it possess you. Learn to "possess your possessions". Don't let the things you own control how you live. For example, if you buy a new boat on credit, you may soon realize that it owns you. It's not just the $300 per month payment, but it's the $100 per month boat slip fee, the $200 per month fuel bill to run it, and the $50 per month insurance bill. Then to top it off, you can only use it 5 months out of the year due to weather! You feel like you have to use it every weekend you can. You skip church, neglect the yard work at home, and before long the boat owns you! I'm not against boats. If you have the cash to buy one and the funds to keep it up, get one. Invite me to go to the lake with you, but make sure you own it and not the other way around.

Don't fall for the get rich quick schemes. Learn to invest for the long haul; use a good financial planner. I suggest one of Dave Ramsey's experienced local providers. Stay focused and don't give up. Most millionaires in America have taken years to get there and have done it on smaller-than-average incomes. They have stayed out of debt, invested steadily, and bought used cars. Discipline is the key to financial success just as it is to success in other areas of our lives.

Learning good financial practices will allow you to enjoy things in life that otherwise you would not have the chance to but, more importantly, it will give you the opportunity to help others, which in turn brings you more joy and blessings! I can't tell you how cool it is to give someone or some organization what they need and have been praying for. It's one of life's greatest joys.

Another benefit of saving for the future is being able to pay for those new tires or that air conditioner when it breaks down! Having 3-6 months of living expenses set aside will totally change your stress level. Dave Ramsey calls this an emergency fund. Some call it a rainy day fund. Whatever you call it, have one. I call it "the being able to sleep at night fund!"

## Chapter Eight
## GETTING BETTER EVERY DAY

Strive to be a better person, a better husband, wife, father, mother, son or daughter, a better employee or employer. Never quit learning. Keep improving.

Understand that perfection is not obtainable. The Bible is full of stories of people who loved God, tried hard, but still were, in our eyes, total screw ups. Take King David, for instance. God called him a "man after God's own heart", yet he committed adultery and had a man killed to cover it up. King Solomon is considered to be the wisest man who ever lived, yet he disobeyed God and married many wives of other religions. Abraham was considered to be the greatest Patriarch of all yet he let his wife, Sara, talk him into having a baby with her maid even though God had promised them that Sara was going to have a baby of their own.

The point is we all mess up. The choice we are faced with is admitting it, asking for forgiveness and moving on or refusing to admit we were wrong, growing bitter and messing up our lives and the lives of those around us. Realize that the "I am" of Jesus is greater than the "I am not" in us. We say "I am not smart enough." Jesus says "I am." We say "I am not good enough" Jesus says "I am." Trust his "I am." He won't let you down.

Read. This seems to be a lost passion. I was taught when I was young to "learn to read and understand what you read, and that there is always a book that will help you learn how to do what you want to do, but you have to be able to read and understand it." I was a freshman in high school when a prominent business man told our class that on a field trip. That was over 40 years ago and I'll never forget it. Turn off the TV, turn off the video games and READ!!

I turned 60 this year. I continue to learn something new each day. I was 50 before I began to understand about God's grace, and about how He loved me no matter what. He has always loved me and never despised me no matter how awful I was. Over the past 10 years I have read dozens of books about His grace. I grew up in church. I am licensed and ordained as a minister, yet through reading about what the early church leaders taught, reading writings by George McDonald, C.S. Lewis, Baxter Krueger, and others, I became aware that even though I was a known leader in the church, my view of God was really messed up. I pray that I will spend the rest of my life learning and teaching others what Jesus showed us about how to live. As I learn more about Him, the better husband, father, grandfather and employer I will become. The most important thing I am learning is that God loves you just as much as He loves me. He sees you through the same eyes He sees me. My job isn't to judge you. My job is to love you! When I do that I'm getting better every day!

## Chapter Nine
## I'M TIRED

Learn to rest. The Bible tells us that God created the Heavens and Earth in six days and rested on the seventh.

The longest of the 10 commandments is number 4. It tells us to remember the Sabbath day and keep it holy. It is to be a time to honor God and thank Him for all He has done for us. It is a time to rest and recharge our bodies.

It is okay to relax and rest. If the world did not stop when God rested, it won't stop when we do. It is not our job to run the world. We will do more by sometimes doing less. Allow your body, mind and soul to rest on a regular basis.

I realize in our society many jobs require us to work on Sundays. Nurses, policeman, retail workers, etc., are required to work some weekends. In that case you are going to need to use one of your days off as your Sabbath. It might be a little more difficult, but you need to be disciplined and make it happen.

Become disciplined about getting up and going to bed at a regular time each day. I realize that there are exceptions, but we need to learn to get up each morning and go to bed each night at the same time. Your body will adjust to a routine and you will begin to sleep better and feel rested.

As a society, we spend countless hours watching TV, Facebooking, and playing video games, which are things that, as a whole, bring absolutely no value to our lives. In fact, many times they become the cause of our not resting well. Our minds can't relax;

we become uptight and unable to rest all over TV programs that aren't real, people we don't like, and games that don't matter. Cut back on these things. Again, like finances, control them. Don't let them control you. Give your burdens to Jesus. In Matthew 11:28, he tells us to "come to Him, give Him our worries, and He will give us rest." Take him up on his offer. There is no other place to find true rest except in Jesus. His mercy and grace are so wonderful if we will accept them. Matthew 11:30 tells us that "His yoke is easy, and the load He gives us is light."

Colossians 2:20-23 tells us that to Jesus it's not about the rules, it's about His Grace and Mercy, so please understand that when I say you need to rest, I'm not talking about a legalistic ritual, I'm talking about the fact that our bodies need rest. I recently read a study about animals at zoos. It appears that if an animal is on display for more than 6 days they become restless and hard to manage. If an animal realizes it needs rest, surely we should be able to do the same! Give it a try.

# Chapter Ten
# WORK IS NOT A DIRTY WORD

For some reason we have gotten the idea that work is a bad thing. Reality is, work is part of what gives us a fulfilling life. We were designed to work. One of the 10 commandments tells us we are to work 6 days and rest 1 day. Working serves several purposes.

1) It gives us money to buy food, shelter and clothing., all of which are nice things to have. As adults these should be things we provide for ourselves, not things we rely upon our parents or the government to give us.

2) It allows us to give to others. As we learned

in chapter four, giving is a vital step to having a Grand and Glorious Life.

3) A good day's work wears us out and causes us to sleep well. Sleep is a vital part of living healthy. We all need around 8 hours of good rest for our bodies to function properly.

4) Work gives us a sense of accomplishment. There is something inside us that makes us feel good about a job well done. When you work, do your best. You will feel better about yourself and whomever you are working for will take notice. As an employer, I can tell you when my employees work hard with a good attitude, I want to reward them. I also know if I don't, someone else will. Hard-working, honest people will always find work. They are a rare commodity in our society.

5) Working hard with a good attitude gives you more control over your destiny. Peo-

ple who don't work, or work but do the minimum required become slaves to their actions. If you do your job well with a good attitude, someone will notice and you will be rewarded.

6) Working keeps our time occupied. Idle time tends to get us in trouble. King David committed adultery largely because he was at home when he was supposed to be at work. Areas that have high unemployment rates typically have high crime rates as well. Not because the people are worse people but because our nature is to fill our time doing something.

7) Working not only benefits us it benefits our community. When I work I am able to buy groceries, tires, gas, etc. from the local stores. When I buy products from the store, the people that work in those stores, restaurants and stations can buy more products from the factories and farms that produce the products. This enables people

to buy things from the company I work for. It's a cycle that benefits everyone in the community.

# Chapter Eleven
# YOU HAVE A DEGREE IN WHAT??

A college degree won't get you a job.

Every time I meet a college student I ask them what they are getting their degree in. I always follow up with what to me seems to be a logical question, "What can you do with that degree?" I would say at least 40% have no idea. I always wonder where are the parents and counselors that allow these kids to get degrees in studies that have no practical application.

The second thing I notice as I talk to young people is that many of them have no personality. They have grown up watching TV, playing video games, and texting on their phones. When it comes time to having a one on one conversation, they are incapable of looking another person in the eye and carrying on a conversation. Parents make your kids put down their games and phones and talk to you. Parents put yours down too. We have a rule at our house and at my company. No phones at meals. Mealtime is a time to eat, relax, and converse. That is what makes us different from animals. Studies show that students who have regular meals with their families have higher SAT scores than other students.

We need to understand that a college degree may get you an interview, but it will not get you a job. You can have a PhD, but if you don't have people skills, no one is going to hire you. Our education system has failed our kids by not teaching them life skills.

Another problem for many college students is that they don't know how to interview.

Here are a few helpful hints.

Guys, before you go to an interview, take a shower, brush your teeth, clean the dirt out from under your fingernails, comb your hair, and put on clean clothes and shoes. I run a construction company. We work in people's homes every day. If you come to my office for an interview, I am going to look at these things. If you haven't combed your hair, washed your hands and your clothes, I am not going to hire you. I already know you are lazy and disrespectful. No use for me to waste my time on you. I know if you won't take care of yourself you won't take care of my customer's homes.

Girls, don't go to an interview dressed seductively. The only person who is going to hire you is a pervert. Dress sharp but modest. Find out before the interview what the appropriate attire is for the company you are interviewing with and go to the interview looking like you could start work today.

Guys and girls, learn to talk. Quit saying "you know" and "like" every other word. Relax, answer the questions, share why you would make a good employee and be quiet. Don't ramble on. Learn to listen. Keep your head up. Make eye contact with your interviewer. Remember in an interview the first impression maybe the only one you get to make.

Also realize it is not important to know everything, so don't act like you do. I would much rather hire someone who doesn't know much about what we do but is eager to learn than to hire someone who acts like they know it all but in reality is all talk. You'll also find other employees will help you more if you are humble and willing to learn.

If you're in high school, I would encourage you to really look at what you want to do in life. If you know, look at the education options. A four year college may be the answer. A tech school might work just as well or better. Going to a local college or getting an online degree might be as good or better than attending a university.

I recently heard an owner of a large tech company say he avoided university students because he felt they were indoctrinated to a point that he could not train them to do the job the way he wanted it done. The point is to know your industry and get the best training you can for the best value.

Another piece of advice that will be helpful is to leave your political views at home. Over the past 10 years this has become a volatile issue. First of all, you are probably like the majority of people in America that are totally ignorant about the view you are presenting. Secondly, you get your facts from the internet, meaning they have a real good chance of being false or at the very least bias. Save your political discussions for the back porch over a beer or glass of wine and learn to listen to all sides. I'm not taking sides with the conservative, progressive, liberal or libertarian side. All sides are guilty of this. Deep down, most of us have the same concerns but we let the media and politicians play us against each other.

# SUMMARY

I love the book of Job. In it we see a great picture of life's ups and downs. We see God's love and mercy. We see our failings and shortcomings. We see that God is in control of the universe. We see how minor of a role we play in the overall picture.

In chapters 38-42, Job is given the opportunity to carry on a conversation with God, and to ask questions and be questioned. Many times I have said that I can't wait to get to heaven and ask God about something that I couldn't understand at the time. Job had this chance. In Job's mind (just like in ours), he thought he was being treated unfairly. After all, he went to church. He prayed. He was a giver. He loved his family and friends. He was a good guy. In Job 1:8 God himself refers to him as the "finest man in all the earth." How would you like to have that on your resume? Still he experienced very tough times.

Job lost his children, his wealth, his stature in the community and his health. His wife urged him to "curse God and die." What a sweetheart. His friends seized the situation to put him down and lift themselves up. He went through "hell" on earth for a period of time. An "aion of kalazo" as Jesus put it in Matthew 25 when referring to the goats, (those that weren't seeing God as he is.) Aion of kalazo would be best translated as "an intense period of correction." (See Rob Bell, Love Win's)

As I mentioned, I have always loved the book of Job and the wisdom and truth that it contains, but I also never understood why Job went through all that he did. It didn't make sense until one day verse 3:25 leapt out at me. I had read the book of Job probably 30-40 times, yet I had never "seen" this verse. Job answers his own question and mine. "What I always feared has happened to me. What I dreaded has come true."

Deep down, Job had always feared losing his status and his wealth. A feeling I think most Americans share. We love our stuff. We think it is where our happiness comes from, but deep down we know it's not the answer. Even though God referred to Job as the "finest man in all the earth," he had his faults just like us. Still, God loved him. Another thing about Job, and maybe the most important thing, was that Job decided to do right without the threat of hell or the promise of heaven. Just like the writer of Ecclesiastes, he realized that doing good didn't always mean there was a reward, but it was still the thing to do. Live life, love your family, enjoy your work. Find your purpose in life. Use your gifts to help those around you in need. Don't overthink it or make it too complicated. I've learned to do that by taking time each morning to listen for God's promptings and asking Him to show me what He's doing in my life and the lives of those around me. Starting the day with a time of quiet reflection rather than a rush out the door to barely make it to work on time calms me and allows me to approach the day with calm and purpose.

There are 4 lessons that I want to leave you with to help you start on your adventure of a "Grand and Glorious Life." Lessons, if learned, will help you achieve the life Jesus promised us all: "Life and that more abundantly."

**Lesson 1**: "We reap what we sow" (Galatians 6:7) Job was sowing seeds of doubt. ("What I always feared most.") This was not a passing thought. Evidently, it was a reoccurring thought. A thought that controlled his life. Something that caused him to fear. II Timothy 1:7 teaches us that "God has not given us the spirit of fear." Don't let fear control you.

Howard Hughes was a germaphobe. Even though he was one of the smartest, richest guys in the world he lived in seclusion the last years of his life because he was afraid of germs! Whatever you fear give it to Jesus. Trust Him to protect you. Give Him your phobias. As my friend Boyce Evens used to say, "Let Go and Let God!"

**Lesson 2**: Bad things sometimes happen to good people. Job was a good man. He did a lot for his family and his community; still, trouble came into his life. We live in a broken world. People sometimes make mistakes and bad choices. We get sick. We wreck our car. Our home burns down. Sometimes disaster is not a "respecter of persons." It's all part of life. As my oldest son says "it's just the part that sucks!"

Just as sure as I am that there is a God who loves me, I know there is a Satan that wants to keep me from enjoying the life God wants me to have. Baxter Kruger once said "Satan's biggest fear is that we will find out who we are." Remember Jesus destroyed Satan's only argument against us when He died on the cross to conquer sin.

Over the years, I have known many good people that have went through tough times, and through no fault of their own, life happened. They lost their job, their spouse or their child died. Their home burnt. These are all things that are part of life. They happen to people of all walks of life. No matter our race, faith or beliefs. They have nothing to do with our religious beliefs or our lack thereof. Don't get me wrong, obviously some of our choices can affect our health, etc. but many things that happen in life are just life. If you're a religious person please don't wonder what sin someone has committed when disaster comes into someone's life. This is what Job's friends did and what I have seen many nosey church people do over the years. Think before you speak. If you can't imagine Jesus saying it you shouldn't say it either.

**Lesson 3** - Never give up: Earlier we learned that Job's wife told him "to curse God and die." I love Job's reply to her in chapter 2 verse 10. "You talk like a foolish woman. Should we accept only good things from the hand of God and never anything bad?" I don't believe God was punishing Job or that He punishes us. I don't believe God sent the troubles into Job's life. The Bible tells us that sin is its own punishment. God is not angry at us about our sin but is anguished over it because He knows how much sin hurts us. That's why He laid down His life, to destroy sins power over us not so He could forgive us. Even though Job was pushed to the brink he never doubted God would ultimately deliver him from his trials. In chapter 19 verses 25-27 he says the following. "But as for me I know that my redeemer lives and He will stand up on the earth at last. And after my body has decayed, yet in my body I will see God! I will see Him with my own eyes. I am overwhelmed at the thought!"

After all Job had gone through he still knew God was enough. If he didn't live through his tough time he was okay with it. He knew there was peace in death. He was content in God's promises. Remember Job lived during Abrahams' time. Two thousand years before Jesus came to earth, yet Job believed the promise God had made about sending a Savior.

**Lesson 4:** Realize that God's plans always exceed our wildest dreams. When we walk in faith and humility, God will do some amazing things in our life.

Remember, Job lost it all. Yet in chapter 42 we see God's redemption at work. In verse 5 Job says, "I had only heard about you before, but now I have seen you with mine own eyes!" In Chapter 42, God tells Job's friends to ask for Job's forgiveness for attacking him during his trials. He instructs Job to forgive them and pray for them. Then in verse 12 we learn that God blessed Job in the second half of his life even more than in the first half. We learn he lived 140 years after this. Verse 17 sums it up. "Then he died an old man who had lived a long full life." What appeared to be a disastrous life to many, ended up being a Grand and Glorious Life, may God grant us the same.

I hope this book will motivate you to take a

new look at your life and where you are headed. I am listing several helpful books that will aid you in your journey. I pray you will take the time to check them out. Grace and Peace! Have a Grand and Glorious Life!

• • •

Hopefully, after reading this book you understand that God wants to be in relationship with us. He loves us. Each religion and denomination has their own ideas of how we make that happen. Most common in the Christian world is the sinners prayer. Surprisingly, this prayer is not in scripture nor in my opinion is it an accurate approach to grace. There are many stories in the New Testament of people who came to understand their need for a relationship with God and none of them prayed a prayer. As they talked with Jesus they felt God's love. If you sense that also, may I suggest you try the following prayer: Father, I thank you for caring so much for me. Thank you for taking away the sins of the world and reconciling the cosmos to yourself. Thank you for promising to make all things new. Thank you for being my Savior and the

Savior of all people! (1 Timothy 4:10). Walk with me each day and help me be aware of what you are doing in the lives of the people around me. Teach me to love like you love. Remember the prayer doesn't save you. Jesus came to be the savior of the world! On the cross He said "It is finished!" Our believing doesn't save us, but it does change our perspective and the way we live. Someone once said that gold doesn't become gold when we find it, but it certainly becomes currency!

# Books and Websites to help you grow

## PERSONAL GROWTH

### Atomic Habits
*James Clear*

### Called to Create
*Jordan Raynor*

## SPIRITUAL GROWTH

### The Bible
*God*

*Get an easy to read version like the New Living Translation, New King James or The Message. Remember the Bible was written in Hebrew and Greek so sometimes the translation into English misses the mark. Doing a little research may help you understand a verse better.*

## Glory Days
*Max Lucado*
*(He has many books All are good!)*

## Jesus and the Undoing of Adam
*Baxter Kruger*

## Spiritual Insanity
*Boyd C. Purcell PhD*

## Love Wins
*Rob Bell*

## In defense of God's love
*The Why Guy (This is a must read!)*

## **PERSONAL FINANCE**

## Total Money Makeover
*Dave Ramsey*

## The Blessed Life
*Robert Morris*

## BUSINESS BOOKS

Thou Shall Prosper
*Rabbi Daniel Lapin*

EntreLeadership
*Dave Ramsey*

## FAITH AND SCIENCE

Amazing Truths
*Michael Guillen*

## CAREER PATH

Start
*John Acuff*

48 Days to the Work You Love
*Dan Miller*

How to be here
*Rob Bell*

## RELATIONSHIPS

From This Day Forward
*Craig and Amy Groeschel*
*(This is also a 5 part series at http://www.life.church/ )*

Boundaries
*Dr. Henry Cloud*

## DAILY DEVOTIONALS

Notes From Papa
*Paul Gray*

Consuming Fire
*George McDonald*

## INSPIRING MESSAGES

thesanctuarydenver.org

Peter Hiett

# ABOUT THE AUTHOR

Brett Neil was born in a small town in Missouri in the late 1950's. During his life he has seen many changes in society but has also seen several repeated patterns. His father died when he was three, leaving him with an empty place in his heart that he tried to fill with everything the world and the church had to offer. In the end this always seemed to leave him frustrated and emptier.

He always knew about God. His mother, brothers and sisters as well as many neighbors loved him and told him about God's love and that God is our Father. The problem was evident. Father's disappear. In his early 20's, he became very involved in church. He was a licensed and ordained pastor, served on every committee possible, and did his best to please his heavenly Father. He did his best to get people saved. This helped, but it still left him empty.

It wasn't until around age 50 that God began to show him the reason he was so empty. He had altogether missed what his heavenly Father was really like. He was not an angry God who couldn't stand to be around him when he messed up, but rather a loving Father that would never leave him or forsake him. A Father that was not angry with him over his sins, but rather was anguished over his sins because of the hurt and pain it caused.

For the past ten years, Brett has done his best to share the love he has found with everyone when given the opportunity.. His prayer is that *Have a Grand and Glorious Day* will help others fill that empty spot in their life.

Visit Brett Neil at
www.grandandgloriousday.com

# HAVE A GRAND & GLORIOUS DAY

Observations from a simple man

BRETT NEIL

CPSIA information can be obtained
at www.ICGtesting.com
Printed in the USA
LVHW021720071121
702687LV00003B/66